First published in 2010 by

Roy Larkin
PO Box 7375
Tadley
RG26 9DS

www.historicroadways.co.uk

© Roy Larkin, 2010

ISBN 978 0 9565014 0 0

Design and typesetting by
Roy Larkin

Printed in England by
Dolman Scott Ltd

LGOC B-type, B43/LN 4743 - 'Ole Bill' ~ RLCM

Contents

Photographic credits

LTM ~ London Transport Museum
RLCM ~ Royal Logistic Corps Museum
MS ~ Mike Sutcliffe, MBE, Collection
RL ~ Roy Larkin Collection
TG ~ Tim Gosling Collection

*Front cover: A column of LGOC B-type buses conveying men of the Warwickshire Regiment
to the First Battle of Ypres in October 1914.
Note the road conditions and consider driving on them with smooth, solid tyres and often in
the dark without lights ~ LTM*

*Back cover: A woman conductor, recruited for the war years, working on
LGOC B-type, B1626/LF 8404, checks the ticket of a soldier back home on leave ~ LTM*

*Daimler, D135, with general service body for the Royal Naval Division
seen outside the LGOC's North Road Coachworks ~ LTM*

Area of Operations on the Western Front

The Front Line had begun to stagnate with few advances by either side by 1915 to broadly follow a line from Niewpoort, past Ypres, Lille, Arras, St Quentin, Soissons and Rheims

LGOC B-type, B5015, LU 8011 ~ LTM

Preface

The British Expeditionary Force arrived in France within days of war being declared against Germany on 4 August 1914. With it came the urgent need to transport hundreds of troops from the French ports to, and around, the battle grounds of Europe.

The London General Omnibus Company stepped into the breach, providing 1,185 buses and lorries for troop and provisions transport in France, Belgium and beyond.

Such was the speed of deployment that there was no time to do anything more than fill the buses with petrol and ship them into Europe. The enduring, even romantic image, of London's buses on the war ravaged roads of France and Belgium in their owner's livery and with myriad adverts remains today.

Nearly a third of the LGOC omnibus fleet was commandeered for wartime service. That in itself was a sizeable contribution. However, the LGOC's cooperation with the War Office at home and abroad spread further than the provision of omnibuses.

Now, through the archives of the Army Service Corps and the London General Omnibus Company, it is possible to tell the true story of London's omnibuses during the Great War and of the LGOC's cooperation with the British War Office in the years leading up to August 1914.

The images are all genuine period photographs and it has to be accepted that the quality is not always that of today's high quality digital images. They are, however, too interesting to omit on the grounds of quality alone.

I am particularly indebted to the staff of the Royal Logistic Corps Museum and the London Transport Museum for their enthusiastic support, access to archives and use of their photographs. Without their help, the story of the LGOC's involvement in Great War would not have been possible.

I am also grateful to the friends who cast expert eyes over the manuscript and my wife, Mary, for her tolerance of my research into the motor transport and logistics of The Great War.

The Wartime Omnibus

LGOC B-type

The Commissioner of Police for the Metropolis issued new regulations regarding motor omnibuses in 1909. These restricted the motor-bus to an unladen weight of 3.5 tons and fully laden weight of 6 tons with no more than 4 tons on the back axle. Maximum seating capacity was for thirty-four passengers.

By this time the London General Omnibus Company (LGOC) had grown, through amalgamation, to a size where large orders for new buses were inevitable. Colonel Frank Searle, LGOC's Chief Engineer, suggested that the company should design and build their own buses at the inherited Vanguard works in Walthamstow. The first

LGOC B-type, B317/LA 9959 on 'Private Hire' with the destination board removed ~ LTM

bus designed and built was the LGOC X-type in 1909. This provided valuable experience in design and production, which led to the LGOC B-type, first produced in 1910.

The designs of both X and B-type owed much to the LGOC's vast experience with numerous different makes with the body differing little from horse-bus days. The merger of the London General Omnibus Company and the Underground Electric Railways

Company of London created the Associated Equipment Company (AEC) as the manufacturing division of the LGOC in 1912.

The B-type thus began a long line of AEC buses designed and built specifically for the streets of London. This tradition lasted to the late 1950s with the introduction of the Routemaster, the last of which were still working London's streets in 2005, with the final ones built in 1968.

Daimler B-type

The Daimler B–type was the result of the agreement between LGOC and Daimler that made Daimler the sole selling agents for B-types built surplus to the LGOC's needs. There was no connection to the German owned Daimler company.

To accommodate Daimler's more powerful, 40hp engine, the B-type chassis was strengthened with side rails 5mm wider and 20mm deeper. They retained the wood/metal sandwich construction of the B-type.

Built by AEC, they carried Daimler badges as it was felt that the LGOC badge was not suitable for buses sold to rivals. The agreement with LGOC continued until December 1917, meaning that the majority of AEC's wartime production was sold to the War Office, initially through Daimler and after AEC came under Ministry of War control, directly to the War Office.

Production of the Daimler continued apace during the war with almost all the chassis built with lorry bodies and used in large numbers for a variety of duties on the Western Front.

The Daimler B-type was often referred to as the D-type due to the fleet numbering system. LGOC B-types were prefixed 'B' and Daimlers prefixed 'D' for the fleet number carried on the bonnet side panels.

Daimler, D253, from the Gearless fleet seen outside Tottenham bus garage in 1913 ~ LTM

Ole Bill seen here at an Armistice Day Parade in the mid-twenties with its commemorative livery ~ LTM

Ole Bill

Built in 1911, LN 4743, 'Ole Bill' is probably the most famous B-type. Commandeered in October 1914, B43 was one of the earliest omnibuses sent to France. Repatriated in 1919 and repurchased by the LGOC, it was refurbished and returned to normal service on London's streets with commemorative brass plaques in recognition of its wartime service.

On 14 February 1920, it was inspected by His Majesty King George V at Buckingham Palace. Here it became the first omnibus ever to be boarded by the King.

Retired from service in the mid-1920s, it was fitted with a new body which commemorated the part played by the bus during the war. It proudly carries the badge of the Royal Army Service Corps (RASC). The Army Service Corps (ASC), who operated the buses in France and Flanders, had received the Royal prefix in 1918 in recognition of the ASC's wartime endeavour. Displaying the names of the great battles of the Great War, Ole Bill was then used for ceremonial duties.

Ole Bill was donated to the Auxiliary Bus Companies Association and appeared regularly at Armistice Day parades and other special events and ceremonies until 1970. The Association presented Ole Bill to the Imperial War Museum on 30 April 1970 where it now resides resplendent in the bright red livery of the 'General' fleet.

11

Ole Bill back working on the streets of London after repatriation and overhaul. The commemorative plaque can be seen below the first window. The brass plate records the years B43 served in France, 1914-1919 with a famous battle recorded for each year. 1919 states simply 'Home' ~ LTM

Ole Bill in the red 'General' livery commemorating the great battles of the First World War on a very wet parade ground while in the stewardship of the Auxiliary Bus Companies Association. The RASC badge is mounted on the front of the body above the driver's canopy ~ RLCM

The roundel on the upper-deck displays an omnibus encircled by 'Ypres - Loos - Somme - Antwerp - Amiens'. Above the windows on both sides are 'Antwerp - Ypres - Ancre - Somme'. All battles served by the omnibus during the Great War ~ RLCM

The War Office Trials

War Office representatives attended the Liverpool Trials of the late 1890s as observers and in 1900 the Mechanical Transport Committee (MTC) was formed to oversee the development of motor transport for military purposes. The first War Office trial was held in 1901 and regular trials, lasting up to a month, were conducted until 1914.

Initially the manufacturers were required to provide a vehicle of their own design, within the parameters set by the MTC. By 1910 the MTC had devised its own specification for what became known as the Subsidy Model Lorry and trials thereafter were accreditation trials, rather than suitability and reliability trials. This was the first motor-lorry designed primarily for military purpose.

All motor vehicles built after 1 January 1910 had to comply with the MTC specification if they were to be admissible into the Subsidy Schemes. These schemes were evolving to encourage private operators to purchase vehicles available for requisition by the War Office in time of 'national need'.

The first instance of any trial for the motor omnibus was in 1908. This was also the first time that any number of normal, everyday working vehicles had been used from a commercial operator.

Previously only a few lorries from working fleets had been hired by the Territorial Force, which later became the Territorial Army, for their annual and weekend training camps. This provided the men with some experience of motor transport without incurring the cost of ownership.

1908 Trials

On 6 December 1908, the first War Office trial involving motor-buses was conducted at Chelmsford, Essex. Two Clarkson steam omnibuses were used to convey men of the 5th Battalion of the Essex Regiment of the Territorial Army for fourteen miles around the Chelmsford area.

The success of this trial led to a more realistic and in-depth trial to be organised for Friday 18 December. The purpose of this trial was for both the military and civilian omnibus operator to learn as much as possible about the viability of the motor omnibus as troop transport, either in peacetime or during wartime at home or abroad.

To this end, the military and civilian roles were kept entirely separate. The buses transported the troops to the direction of the Commanding Officers, with the operation of the buses left to the LGOC.

Captain R.K. Bagnall-Wilde, Royal Engineers and the Secretary of the Mechanical Transport Committee of the War Office was the organising officer. Lieutenant-General Sir Arthur Paget was the War Office observer. Frank Searle of the LGOC took command of the civilian role.

In order to make the trial as realistic as possible, a scenario was devised by the War Office whereby an invading army had landed on the banks of the river Crouch in Essex. The invaders (who quickly became German in the imagination of those taking part) were presumed to be heading across country to Shoeburyness, whose defences were deemed to be undermanned. A body of troops had therefore to be conveyed to the area as quickly as possible.

The nearest available troops were at Warley Barracks, near Brentwood, Essex and the motor-buses were assembled from various LGOC garages in London. In recognition that this was the first trial on such a scale, the LGOC had been given several days notice that they would be required to provide adequate transport for the number of troops.

Frank Searle, chief engineer of the amalgamated General, Vanguard Motorbus Company and London Road Car fleets took personal command, assembling his own team of assistants from LGOC staff members. They were,

Mr Field, the new assistant chief; Mr Fenner, who was head of the hiring department; Mr Pollard, of the Road Car division; Mr Turner-Smith, in charge of Vanguard's rolling stock and Mr Johnson, who was responsible for eliminating wasted journeys. Searle followed the day's events in his own car, accompanied by Colonel Cobbett of the Norfolk Territorials and a reporter from The Commercial Motor as interested spectators.

The three amalgamated companies, General, Vanguard and Road Car, were required by Searle to muster eight omnibuses each at Upton Park garage at 5.30am on the Friday morning. In addition, each supplied a breakdown tender of the same make as the buses. These tenders carried spare parts,

One of the earliest to display the 'General' name, this de Dion, LC 919, was photographed in January 1906 outside St James Norlands parish church, West London ~ LTM

M-type de Dions, M7 and M10, seen here in 1912. It is not recorded whether it was this model de Dion used for the trial or the earlier model seen on the previous page ~ LTM

grease, oil, petrol and general stores. All the vehicles were to be made ready for a hard day of working.

The General used 30hp de Dions; Vanguard, Milnes-Daimlers and Road Car provided 40hp Straker-Squires. The Daimlers had been stripped of their service numbers and route boards, whereas the Straker-Squires and de Dions still carried their everyday route boards, such as 'Hammersmith and Shoreditch' and 'Liverpool Street and Barnes'. What the local population of Essex made of the advertised routes and destinations is open to conjecture.

The journey from Upton to Warley was undertaken in thick fog and it was noted that the bright acetylene lights of

the Milnes-Daimlers hindered rather than helped the Vanguard drivers. Divided into three columns, each was headed by a driver who was familiar with the roads leading out of London.

With each company forming a column, it was perhaps inevitable that an element of competition would impinge on proceedings. Each column seemed determined to be first to reach Warley, despite Searle's attempts to restore order once he had realised what was happening. Two Daimlers arrived first, followed by a de Dion and it was obvious, from the order that the rest arrived, that a fair amount of passing and re-passing had been going on throughout the journey. This was despite the foggy conditions and drivers unfamiliar with the roads.

At Warley, four companies of the 1st Norfolk and one company of the 7th Essex Territorials had been assembled outside the barracks. They were split into two columns, one commanded by Lieutenant Colonel Massey and the other by Major Ballard, both of the 1st Norfolk Regiment. Lieutenant General Sir Arthur Paget was appointed by the Mechanical Transport Committee as the military observer.

The men lined up in detachments of twenty-five at twenty yard intervals along the road ready for embussing. All of the men carried full battle kit, with blankets and rations for one day.

Half of the men carried 150 rounds of ammunition and half carried ninety rounds plus entrenching spades and picks. Each bus carried 100 rounds of spare ammunition per man and spare

rations while a Maxim Gun was carried on every eighth vehicle. Searle's original three columns were divided into two and lined up, ready for embussing at 8.30am.

The two columns, under instruction from the commanding officers, followed different routes to Shoeburyness. Lt Col Massey took the route via Horndon, Orsett, Stanford and Pitsea and Major Ballard took the more northerly Billericay, Crag's Hill, Wickford and Rayleigh route. This redistribution of the columns resulted in two columns of mixed makes and the use of two routes further added to the difficulty of assisting breakdowns.

Two different routes were chosen to follow standard military practice when moving large columns, particularly on narrow country routes. This ensured

A Milnes-Daimler from the Vanguard company ~ LTM

An obviously posed Milnes-Daimler, possibly on a private hire excursion ~ LTM

that should one route be blocked for any reason that the progress of the entire movement was not compromised.

One of the Straker-Squire breakdown wagons was abandoned, with its load, at Warley when a sprocket shaft twisted off behind the chain pinion. This reduced the number of breakdown tenders to one for each column. By some misunderstanding, blamed on the driver, both the remaining breakdown tenders accompanied column number one, which comprised Daimlers and Straker-Squires. It was fortunate that this was the only column to have any serious problems.

An indication of the road conditions is that wide tracks were left by the twin rear wheels, which left the surface badly cut up. While this made it easy

for the following members of the columns to follow the route, it also meant that four buses from column one slipped off the road into ditches, requiring the assistance of the breakdown crews to recover them back onto the road.

One bus from column two, was also ditched, but extricated itself without the need to redirect the breakdown tender following the wrong column. Of the five buses ditched, three were Daimlers and two were Straker-Squires. None of the de Dions were ditched, which was attributed to their lighter construction.

All five of the ditchings were caused by the driver moving too far to the left and onto soft ground while trying to pass oncoming vehicles. This particular problem was quickly solved by the convoys not venturing far from the crown of the road for the rest of the day. This lesson was later incorporated into regulations for convoys during the war years. On the return journey, one of the Daimlers broke through the road surface, sinking to its axles.

The two columns converged at Hadleigh Cross Roads soon after midday, where the troops were disembarked and immediately embussed for the return journey. The return journey is reported as without mishap and Warley barracks were reached at 5.00pm.

The experiment was deemed a success. Both the LGOC and Captain Bagnall-Wilde learned valuable lessons, particularly as there had

purposely been no collusion between the two. Journey times were relatively slow, and this was considered due to the shepherding of columns along unfamiliar roads with the foggy conditions and the persistent rain creating a poor road surface. It was noted that times would be quicker if the drivers had the opportunity to rehearse driving on unfamiliar country roads, rather than the urban roads they were more familiar with.

The MTC report reveals that an average speed of 12mph should be possible in good conditions, reducing to 9mph in poor conditions. These speeds would appear to be somewhat optimistic for the time, possibly because the MTC felt the need to impress the War Office in Whitehall with the value of motor transport.

A chain drive Straker-Squire from the London Road Car Company ~ LTM

The report noted that the omnibus was well suited to carrying walking wounded from front lines and that they could be converted to lorry bodies for the carriage of field guns and ammunition. The recommendation for further trials appears not to have been taken up as the omnibus is not mentioned in any further War Office MTC reports until 1912.

A report from the LGOC was requested by the MTC and published in the 1908 Annual Report of the MTC. Written by Wilfrid Dumble, it remarks that the anticipated problems of overheating on long journeys and steep hills did not materialise and that radiators and water circulation proved quite efficient. An MTC note states: 'Overheating was observed and considerable delays due to loss of water was experienced'.

The aggregate mileage for the day was 2,400 miles and the trial was completed within fifteen hours with every bus returned to its garage in good mechanical order. The report suggested that routes be clearly defined, especially if diversions were needed as 'the sense and geography of our men is distinctly lacking in the absence of familiar landmarks'.

The routes showed the importance of columns comprising a single make where possible, as the speed of the column was determined by the slowest vehicle. Mixing fast and slow vehicles proved a hindrance and the lower powered buses slowed the entire column, especially on the hills.

It was also noted that a gap of sixty yards should be maintained between vehicles. This would even out the column speed when differences in the speed of individual vehicles was

created by circumstance, such as gear changing, gradients etc.

The ditching of some buses showed that a spare vehicle in every eight in the column would quickly enable troops to transfer buses in the event of accident. This would mean all the troops would arrive with the column, instead of some time later, after their particular vehicle had been rescued.

It was noted that the omnibus body was not convenient for carrying troops and their equipment, though was entirely suitable for carrying troops alone. It was also recorded that a standing order of 'no smoking or spitting while on the bus' should be in place at all times.

1912 Trial

By 1912, the Subsidy lorry had largely proved its reliability. The trial held between 9 and 29 August was therefore intended more as a comparison between makes than to prove reliability or suitability. The vehicles would have been driven by their usual civilian drivers accompanied by observers from the War Office.

The opportunity was taken to include omnibuses as a direct comparison with the motor lorry. The Mechanical Transport Committee at the War Office made it clear that the buses and lorries were not in competition with each other and that the trial was purely to find out how they compared for the work envisaged by the military.

Roads varying from city roads to country lanes including gradients as steep as 1 in 6 comprised the trial with the buses being introduced on the 26 August. A Leyland ST-type, 30hp,

Driver, Mr Emmanuel Whitehead stands proudly with his B-type, B624/LE 9174 ~ LTM

was hired from The New Central Omnibus Company, which was formerly the London Central Omnibus Company and two LGOC B-types from the LGOC.

The companies were informed of the road conditions, including the routes and gradients. They were required to provide the buses with a load of sandbags to represent the carrying capacity of each bus.

When the buses assembled at the start, the MTC suggested to the bus companies that they were greatly over estimating the load their buses could carry. The bus companies remained adamant that their vehicles were very capable of carrying the load.

The trial began and the loads were gradually decreased until they reached 30-cwt when the MTC lost patience and exempted the buses from the steepest hills on the route.

The over optimism by Central is more understandable than the LGOC, who were well aware of the carrying capacity of the B-type. The LGOC had been forced into building single-deck B-types for their hillier routes as the double-deckers were unable to climb the hills with a full load of passengers.

In the report of the trial, the MTC were quick to comment that the omnibus was designed for a very particular purpose. It was unacceptable to expect a vehicle designed to work on the streets of London to be capable of the same work as a vehicle designed to meet specific military requirements.

Despite having the same size engine as the subsidy lorry, the buses suffered from a lower performance than the lorry. The rear axle ratios were too high to allow climbing of steep hills and the cooling systems were inadequate for heavy work. The worm drive rear axle of the B-type was deemed unsuitable other than for the stop/start London street work.

The chain drive in the gearbox of the B-type was accepted as being ideal for the stop/start journeys it was designed for but unsuitable for long rural journeys. The brakes were poor on both buses, particularly on the B-type, which required 150 yards to stop on the steeper downhill sections.

The Leyland bus was regarded as a superior vehicle to the B-type, though no more suited to the rigours of military work. The bus still fell short of the capabilities of the Class B subsidy lorry by the same maker.

To produce an accurate comparison for petrol consumption that allowed for the different carrying capacity of the different classes, the gross ton miles per gallon was calculated. Average speeds were measured on both main and hilly routes, though only the hilly routes were recorded for the buses.

It was the gross ton miles per gallon that most interested the MTC. The advantage of the 3-ton Class A subsidy lorries was obvious. It was comparing the 30-cwt Class B lorry and the 30-cwt omnibuses that convinced the MTC of the need for vehicles built specifically

Leyland ST.30hp with Brush 34-seat body, new in August 1912 ~ MS

Thornycroft J-type 3-ton Class A subsidy lorry ~ RL

for their own needs. The report concluded that whilst the omnibus was well suited for the streets of London, it was wholly unsuited to the needs of the military. There was no intended criticism of the omnibus in its own environment, only recognition that the omnibus was as unsuitable for the requirements of the military as the subsidy lorry was for the particular and very different needs of the London bus operators.

Results of the 1912 Trial from Mechanical Transport Committee Records

Make and Type	Average Speed on Hilly Routes (mph)	Gross Ton Miles per Gallon
Leyland Class A	11.8	59.2
Thornycroft Class A	10.6	49.1
Leyland Class B	13.4	50.6
Leyland Bus	12.9	41.2
LGOC B-type	12.5	39.3

The Western Front

The 1,185 omnibuses commandeered by the War Office in 1914 and 1915 represented nearly one third of the LGOC's General fleet. That such a large proportion was commandeered was of the LGOC's own making.

B-types new to the General fleet in 1913 and 1914 complied with the entirely voluntary Subsidy Scheme and as such were registered with the War Office. The scheme encouraged owners to buy new vehicles and properly maintain them, providing a pool of vehicles that could be called on by the War Office in time of 'national need'.

The subsidy scheme was for Class A (3-ton) and Class B (30-cwt) vehicles. No record has been found as to what class the B-type was registered, but it is almost certain that they were Class B.

Lieutenant A. M. Beatson, ASC, who commanded a company allotted to the 1st Indian Cavalry Supply Column, wrote that his LGOC buses had been converted to general service lorry bodies before leaving Grove Park and that they were 30-cwt capacity. The 1912 War Office trial had also shown the B-type only had 30-cwt capacity.

The terms of the scheme offered little inducement for many owners. For the LGOC, who built and maintained their vehicles in-house, the subsidy scheme provided a useful extra revenue stream. LGOC knew that registered vehicles would be commandeered first and that up to one third of their fleet could be lost to the military with only 3 day's notice.

The first of the LGOC fleet commandeered for overseas service were thirty single-deck, 20-seat, B-type omnibuses from the General fleet. Built just a few months earlier, they were commandeered on 1 August 1914, three days before Britain entered the war. Stripped of their interiors and

Men from the ASC pose in April 1915. Note the surviving destination board and the newly painted destination ~ LTM

Crews pose with their converted ambulances. The central figure appears to be a senior naval officer suggesting they were destined for the Admiralty ~ LTM

fittings, they were hastily converted into ambulances, arriving in Dover the same night for shipment to France. There is no further record of these buses, although the assumption would be that they were destined for Belgium and were either captured or destroyed by the Germans, probably at Antwerp.

In early September 1914, the Admiralty requested the loan of omnibuses for use in Flanders. Seventy D-type Daimlers were handed over to the Naval Brigade from the Tramways Omnibus Company (MET) and the Gearless Motor Omnibus Company fleets. They were not subsidy scheme registered and it seems that the LGOC saw their loan as an opportunity to reduce the number of non-standard buses in the LGOC fleet by sending buses from the associated companies that operated different makes to the General's B-type.

They were shipped to Dunkerque in their blue livery and advertisements. With volunteer crews they looked just as they had on the streets of London.

Formed into a new unit of the Royal Marines, they initially advanced to Antwerp before most were lost to the enemy in the subsequent retreat. The survivors from Antwerp were used to carry a battalion of London Scottish troops to the First Battle of Ypres on 21 October 1914.

This operation confirmed that the ordinary omnibus could serve as a troop carrier and in October a further 300 buses were pressed into military service at short notice. All the LGOC drivers that volunteered from this time were enrolled into the Army Service Corps for the duration of the war.

The unit was later taken over from the Navy and became the 16th Auxiliary Omnibus Company, attached to the Fifth Army, based in the northern French town of St Omer.

Immediately after arriving in France, the red and white livery of the General fleet was initially painted over in grey and later khaki. Lorries were also initially painted grey although khaki was quickly adopted as it provided better camouflage on open ground.

The glass was removed from the windows which were boarded up with planks nailed to the sides. The windows were vulnerable to the men's packs and rifles and only occasionally broken by enemy shellfire.

Seventy-five of the buses had their bodies cut off at window level to be converted into lorries on arrival at Rouen. Buses commandeered at later dates had their bodies removed entirely and replaced by general service bodies at the LGOC's North Road Coachworks in North London before being taken over by the War Office.

These 300 vehicles were formed at Grove Park, the ASC mobilisation and training centre near Lewisham in South East London. Formed as 1st, 2nd, 3rd and 4th Auxiliary Omnibus

MET Daimlers, seen in Ghent assisting with the evacuation of Belgian refugees. The lack of damage indicates they had not been in Belgium many days ~ LTM

Royal Naval Division Daimlers at Boulogne in the autumn of 1914. Already their resplendent London livery has been replaced by drab military grey ~ LTM

Companies, each with seventy-five vehicles, they were allocated Army Service Corps Company numbers, 90, 91, 92 and 93 respectively.

Three of the companies were composed of LGOC and ASC drivers and the fourth was made up from specially enlisted men. 1 and 2 Companies were kept as the originally formed omnibus companies, 3 Company became a General Head Quarters Ammunition Park and 4 Company was converted in France to ordinary general service lorries for various duties and later its headquarters and workshop facilities became a Mobile Repair Unit.

Originally regarded as loans to the government, the requisitioned buses were converted to sales on 11 October 1914. On that date, thirty single-deck General omnibuses, ninety-four double-deck B-types, 219 MET Daimlers and twenty-two Gearless Daimlers are recorded as sales. Six MET Daimlers, previously on loan to Manchester Corporation were sold to the War Office on 31 October 1914.

Seventy of the Daimlers were retained as buses and the remainder were rebodied as general service lorries. The LGOC kept the bus bodies in store for future use.

During the last two weeks of October, 420 B-types were commandeered and by March 1915, a further 351 buses had been requisitioned from the General fleet. An additional forty-one buses from associated companies, including at least ten Leylands from the Bedford garage of the by now

LGOC owned New Central Omnibus Company, had also joined the military by March. There is no record of any further buses being commandeered after March 1915.

In October 1915, 200 buses were returned by the War Office, apparently at the LGOC's request. No details have been found although 200 LGOC men from the Royal Naval Transport Division returned to London at the same time.

The War Office had realised that hundreds of impressed vehicles were no good without drivers and therefore the driver was regarded as part of the vehicle. In practice, this appears not to have been enforced with only volunteer LGOC drivers being required to remain with their vehicles.

Only half of the buses taken to France had LGOC drivers, the other half were collected from LGOC garages as they returned at the shift end by ASC drivers from Grove Park. These later requisitions were converted to wartime livery with shuttered windows before leaving Grove Park for Avonmouth docks and on to foreign fields.

1st Auxiliary Omnibus Company, commanded by Major S.W. Morrison, ASC, left Grove Park on 17 October 1914. They stopped overnight at Marlborough and arrived at Avonmouth on 18 October with seventy-five buses, four motor cars and two lorries, one of which was a mobile workshop lorry.

They arrived at Rouen on 23 October, moved to Blangy-sur-Bresle and were

LGOC B-types at Grove Park shown in military guise prior to departure to Avonmouth docks en-route for France ~ RLCM

A column of LGOC B-types attached to 52 Coy ASC convey troops from the 1st Indian Cavalry on a typically narrow dirt road in France. It was easy to slip from the narrow road and become bogged down in the muddy verges ~ LTM

attached to the Second Army. Their first work was to carry 600 men of the Seaforth Highlanders, Royal Warwicks and Royal Dublins from St Venant to Houplines, near Armentieres, during the First Battle of Ypres.

2nd Auxiliary Omnibus Park, commanded by Captain Coulson, ASC, left Grove Park on 22 October 1914, spent the night at Hampton Court and arrived at Avonmouth docks on 23 October. One bus was wrecked en-route when in collision with a lamp standard in Bristol.

The company arrived at Rouen between 27 and 29 October and travelled to Bailleul where they were attached to

the First Army. Their first duty was to move 1,000 French infantry to Elverdinge on 3 November and then 1,800 men of the French Chasseurs Alpins on the 12 November.

In 1915, the 15th Auxiliary Omnibus Company was formed and attached to the Third Army. Two further companies were formed in December 1916, these being 50th and 51st Auxiliary Omnibus Companies.

The 18th Auxiliary Omnibus Company was formed in 1916 and attached to the Fourth Army to cope with the ever increasing workload. This company was issued with Locomobile lorries which had been sold by America to

MET Daimlers convey the London Scottish on a muddy pavé road to the First Battle of Ypres in October 1914 ~ LTM

The roads of Flanders were of Belgian pavé, seemingly designed to shake every chassis bolt loose and shatter road springs. In wet weather they became notoriously slippery and there are numerous reports of the difficulty in keeping vehicles from sliding off the road. Almost constant shelling during times of battle destroyed roads and ASC records tell of lorries 'sinking into the mud to the bottom of their bodies'.

Road Inspector, A. Chouffot, who later became a Sergeant Major, ASC, was fulsome in his praise of LGOC drivers in coping with the conditions in September 1915;

'It was really amazing how they ever, during last winter kept their buses, in the dark without lights, in a narrow pavé road covered with two or three inches of grease'.

Northern France was a largely rural area with few metalled roads. Most were little more than single width dirt tracks worn by centuries of farm cart traffic. These turned to mud in the wet, to dust in dry spells and quickly deteriorated with the extra burden of motor transport.

Whether the dust or the mud was preferable to the other is a moot point. Both impregnated everything, men and

Germany and then been captured en-route by the Royal Navy. With characteristic humour, the Iron Cross was designated as the unit sign and painted on the vehicles.

Road conditions were testing, with the Auxiliary Omnibus Park diary stating;

'Wind and rain were very violent, rendering the vehicles keeping on the pavé very difficult. Delays through vehicles being ditched. Roads terribly bad and encumbered by Cavalry and Artillery. Windows of certain vehicles (including the OC's car) shattered by concussion of firing.'

machines alike. The dust choked in summer, the mud clung to clothing in winter, meaning the men lived and worked in cold, wet clothes.

One can only imagine how cold the drivers must have been in an open-cabbed bus or lorry in muddy, wet clothing in the icy winds of winter. At least the bitter cold helped keep the lice population down.

Private H. Adcock, serving with 3 Field Ambulance in Northern France, recalls in March 1915, that he saw the MET Daimlers regularly and that it was impossible to see much of them for the mud that covered them.

During thaw conditions, all motor transport was banned from using the roads. This was partly because they rapidly became choked with stranded vehicles but mainly it was to prevent further deterioration of the already poor surfaces.

Congestion was a major problem with narrow roads shared by all, including the local population. Attempts to alleviate congestion included designating roads as directional, thereby creating a round trip circuit and also by allocating roads for specific use. Motor transport could only use roads permitted to it, as could horse transport and infantry, which worked well in theory.

In practice, roads became impassable through shell damage, the weather, obstructions such as breakdowns and

LGOC B-type used as an ambulance by 93 Coy ASC seen collecting walking wounded from somewhere on the Somme ~ LTM

A column of Daimlers with general service bodies at a lorry park alongside a road repairing Labour Corps Company ~ RLCM

the general confusion of a battle area so that the roads were often shared by all. Traffic Control records give an indication of the congestion and the pounding the roads received. On 21 July 1915, seven weeks after the Battle of the Somme started, the following traffic passed through Fricourt, a village at the heart of the Somme battlefield.

Soldiers – 26,536.
Horse and rider – 5,000+
Horse drawn wagons – 3,000
Motor Lorries – 813
Motor cycles – 617
Motor cars – 568
Motor ambulances – 330

Roads needed constant repair and maintenance by the Royal Engineers, assisted by the ASC Labour Corps and often the passing traffic was used to roll road stone into the surface. The working environment for drivers in

France or Flanders certainly bore no relation to the streets of London.

Every driver was issued with a copy of *Drivers' Orders* drawn up by the Army Service Corps, which had to be carried at all times when on duty. They detailed the responsibilities of the drivers and were rigorously enforced by the military police and local gendarmes loaned by the French government to support the small British military police force.

Speed limits were particularly rigorously controlled to minimise wear to both road and vehicle. The speed limit for lorries and buses was 10mph on the open road and 6mph through towns and villages. Lorries were to drive to the right at all times, though keeping to the crown of the road to avoid sinking into the soft edges. Each vehicle had a crew of two who were responsible for the cleanliness, routine maintenance and equipment, such as spades and non-slip chains.

Convoys, or columns, which could exceed one hundred vehicles and often exceeded fifty, operated under *Traffic Orders – Army Routine Orders.* Although drawn up and issued by individual armies, they were essentially the same with only slight changes depending on individual circumstance. These supplemented and took precedence over the ASC *Drivers' Orders.* Different orders applied to different classes of vehicle with omnibuses included in the 'over 3-ton' class and regarded as lorries for the purpose of the orders. It is a sign of the unfamiliarity of the motor vehicle to the military that convoys were 'marched' and not driven.

Every twelfth vehicle had to carry a red disc to the rear and the following vehicle was not permitted to be closer than fifty yards to it. This was to allow overtaking by cars and motorcyclists, who 'shepherded' the column, in an effort to keep it intact. Speed limits were slightly lower, being 8mph on the open road to help ensure there were no stragglers. Columns were not to be parked on soft ground, in towns or in any way to cause obstruction to other road users.

For the men, their bus was also their home. Initially, there were no billets

A column of LGOCs with general service bodies at rest on a dirt road near Albert in 1916. Note the width of the road and poor condition of the road-edges ~ RLCM

MET Daimlers in a Belgian town. The condition of the buses and the civilian population indicate the early days of the Great War, probably mid-September 1914 ~ LTM

available, so they slept on board, storing their belongings in old petrol cans. As the war progressed, billets were available at the larger bases.

In rural towns, private houses provided rooms that were hired for the officers while the men were accommodated in town halls. More often motor transport would be parked away from the town and the danger of shelling. Columns were parked at the roadside, if the road was wide enough, or on hastily laid hardstanding that was often no more than railway sleepers alongside the road and where the vehicles could be covered with camouflage.

It is worth remembering that, only a matter of weeks before, those who now found themselves in the thick of war, were just ordinary working men who chose to volunteer for King and country. They were far removed from the professional soldier of today.

Neither should the men's families be forgotten. Their head of the family went to work as normal, but instead of returning home that evening might have volunteered with his workmates. By evening, he might be enlisted into the army and possibly en-route to Avonmouth Docks and France. The only inkling as to when they would return was the widely held belief that the war would be over by Christmas.

One can only imagine how the men, wives, children, girlfriends and parents felt about volunteering for King and country. No doubt very patriotic and with a sense of adventure, but also great anxiety, at least in private.

Private Edward Darby, ASC, recounts in his diary, *How to Become a Soldier in One Month*, his early army days. He volunteered at 10.00am on 19 October 1914 at the Whitehall Recruiting Centre and within hours, along with forty others, was at Grove Park.

After passing his medical he was kitted out and given his regimental number and pay book, which included one day's pay. Now in uniform, he was told by a 'Brass Hat' that he was 'in the army now' and sent to an unnamed London bus garage. Here, buses were taken over as they returned from service and driven to Grove Park to be parked in the street for the night.

On the morning of 20 October the buses were filled with petrol, stores and large tins of grey paint before setting off to Ascot Racecourse where they spent the night. Here he was able to buy a postcard to inform his fiancée of what had happened. The following day the company moved to Marlborough, parked in the main street and was told by the Sergeant Major that they embarked for France from Avonmouth the following day.

This surprised Private Darby who recalled that they were a mix of lorry, omnibus, taxi drivers and various other tradesmen, some with only a vague notion about driving. Darby was a chauffeur/mechanic and presumably had not envisaged that volunteering meant going to France within just a couple of days.

On 22 October they embarked on an old tramp steamer bound for Rouen. The men underwent basic musketry and arms drill while waiting for the buses to be loaded aboard ship by the Avonmouth dockers.

LGOC, B251/LA 9839, with general service body and War Department number, 3752. The 'non-skids' on the rear wheels were necessary on the poor roads and it was the driver's responsibility to ensure they were with the vehicle before starting a journey ~ RL

Soldiers embussing at an unknown location. Wooded areas provided welcome cover from enemy aircraft ~ LTM

They arrived in Rouen in the morning of 25 October and were promptly sent on a four-hour route march as compensation for being cooped up on ship for several days. On their return, they discovered several Frenchmen sawing the top decks from their buses, effectively turning them into lorries. By late afternoon they were on their way to the Front, reaching Abbeville before stopping overnight. The following day they moved on to St Omer and then to Hazebrouck to join the 2nd Cavalry Division Supply Column and, within a fortnight of volunteering, Darby had left civilian life to be in the thick of war.

While attached to their respective armies, the companies worked directly for the army as independent units with no central organisation supervising their operations. The workload was heavy with each army showing great reluctance to withdraw vehicles from service for maintenance or even inspection. One, unnamed, army even requested that the crews be doubled in strength so that the buses could be run continuously, seven days a week.

This meant that the condition of the vehicles suffered greatly and it is a tribute to the B-type that they remained capable of working. By December 1916, the vehicles of the 2nd and 16th Companies were virtually incapable of further work and those of 15th and 18th Companies were in need of complete overhaul.

Allocating bus companies to particular armies meant that they operated on a local basis, usually in isolation. There could be no quick response to any particular army in need of additional transport, and armies were reluctant to release transport to other armies and leave themselves short.

This situation resulted in the formation of the Auxiliary Omnibus Park, which withdrew the vehicles from individual army control to that of GHQ. Formed in December 1916, it was the spring of 1917 before the reorganisation was complete, under the command of Lt Col G.L.H. Howell, ASC, who had been transferred from 13th Corps Ammunition Park.

The reorganisation allowed the more efficient use and planning of resources. It also allowed monitoring of the mechanical condition and the ability to withdraw vehicles, in rotation, for repair and servicing or overhaul. The Auxiliary Omnibus Park consisted of seven companies comprising 650 vehicles and 18,000 men with a carrying capacity of 13,300 men with their equipment.

Various reports exist by the drivers in France of how well their individual buses performed, often stating that they went the entire war without repair or need for workshop time. While there is no doubt that the buses performed admirably, this might be an

Troops boarding buses on the way to the Front ~ RLCM

Battle-worn Daimler on a wooden road, probably in Flanders. Wooden roads were built when the conditions made travel otherwise impossible ~ RLCM

understandably rosier picture than the reality. ASC records indicate that after the forming of the Auxiliary Omnibus Park, all vehicles were routinely serviced and overhauled. Considering the mileages covered and the road conditions it would be a remarkable achievement if any of the relatively primitive vehicles did not need overhauling during four years of service in France and Flanders.

Twenty-five of the original complement of seventy-five vehicles were left under the direct control of each army with fifty allotted to the Omnibus Park. The Omnibus Park was established at St Valery-sur-Somme, where all the vehicles were overhauled and the lorries fitted with seats. Vehicles

deemed too badly damaged for repair at the unit's workshops were sent to No.3 Repair Shop at St Omer.

This was based in the old jute factory, alongside the canal and had workshop facilities to completely overhaul thirty vehicles per week, which was greater capacity than most manufacturers at the time. Incoming vehicles were assessed and allocated one of the 300 bays in the workshops. They were stripped of bodies and mechanical parts, which were refurbished by specialist mechanics.

Engines, axles and gearboxes were returned to new condition and bench tested before the chassis was reassembled with a test body for a lengthy road test with a full load. Only after the vehicle was certified as being in the same condition as when new was the original refurbished body refitted and the vehicle passed as fit for service.

New omnibus companies were formed and as vehicles were made serviceable they were returned to work for whichever army had the greatest need. The Auxiliary Omnibus Park subsequently moved to Frevent to be more central before moving again to the Ypres Salient in 1917 for the Third Battle of Ypres. During the British advance of 1918, the Omnibus Park was stationed at intervals along the Doullens-St Pol-Bethune-Ypres road.

Each army provided the Auxiliary Omnibus Park with a Movement Order detailing the troops to be moved and the route. The Omnibus Park would then provide the number of buses and lorries to facilitate the troop movement.

Each omnibus carried twenty-five men and each converted lorry twenty men. These lorries were not cut down buses but had general service bodies with seating for twenty. The lower decks of buses allowed sixteen seats and 3-ton lorries carried the troops' kit.

The mainstay of the workload was transporting troops and working parties to and from the frontline trenches. Troops were rotated, meaning they only spent a few days or sometimes a week in the frontline. They otherwise spent their time behind the lines, either at rest or training.

Daimlers from the MET and Gearless fleets share the road with foot soldiers, civilians and cars in a busy Belgian town, believed to be Ostend ~ LTM

38

Troops preparing to embus Royal Naval Division Daimlers on a pavé road somewhere in Flanders during the autumn of 1914 ~ LTM

This rotation provided daily trips to the front with fresh men and returning with men due to be relieved and walking wounded.

At all times a complement of buses was kept ready at one hour notice to provide transport for armies needing to move troops into battle at the start of any new offensive, or to strengthen the lines during enemy offensives. The pooling of the buses into the Auxiliary Omnibus Park allowed buses to be sent to where they were needed most as well as providing repair facilities.

Buses and crews not required for routine daily trips to the front were not kept idle. Apart from the opportunity afforded for maintenance, they were used on training exercises for troop movements. This ensured that the

Park drivers were well-practised in their role and troops gained experience in embussing and debussing.

This training meant that embussing could be achieved as efficiently as possible. Auxiliary Omnibus Park records show that the time needed to embus a Brigade of 3,500 men varied from six to fifteen minutes, though the speediest embussing during training was as little as four and a half minutes.

One troop movement in July 1917 involved the use of ninety-two buses plus two spare and fifty-three lorries with two spares. The troops were divided into groups of twenty-five and twenty before being stationed at intervals alongside the road at the embussing point. When the buses arrived, the men were already waiting to board their allotted bus. This was the same procedure that had been first tested at Hadleigh Cross Roads during the 1908 Trial.

On 28 January 1917, twenty-five buses from 16th Auxiliary Omnibus Company were attached to No.5 Mobile Repair Unit (803 Coy ASC) for maintenance and repairs. This was to relieve the pressure on the company's own workshops. They had all seen heavy service during the Somme operations and were in very poor condition with some needing towing to workshops which had been established at Beauval.

These buses were used to convey troops and working parties to the front lines, usually at night and at all times there were two buses in workshops for maintenance and repair. As each was returned to service it was replaced with the next most needy, thereby rotating the buses in a continual maintenance programme. Breakdowns were accommodated by the workshops as and when they occurred.

Buses were allotted to ASC Motor Ambulance Companies to assist with the evacuation of patients from Casualty Clearing Stations behind the lines to hospitals and from hospitals to the ports for repatriation. There is no evidence that buses were used as ambulances from the trenches to the Casualty Clearing Stations.

812 (MT) Coy ASC was formed on 11 November 1916 as the 41st Auxiliary Ambulance Car Company to consolidate the various ambulance companies working in the Rouen area. Based at the Audax Motor Works in Rouen, the company strength of seventy-three ambulances included thirteen omnibuses, comprising three Daimlers, seven LGOC B-types, two Straker-Squires and one Dennis. The Dennis and Straker-Squires were probably donations.

Troops embus on a narrow street in a Flemish town ~ LTM

A MET Daimler being used as an ambulance. The cleanliness of both bus and patients suggests a posed photograph ~ LTM

a further four buses were taken over on 4 April 1917. Based at Cayeux they conveyed convalescents from Cayeux to Noyelles-sur-Mer station for return to active service. In September, five more buses were allotted to assist with the growing workload in the Abbeville area. The buses were used to complement the forty ambulances of various makes already operated by the company.

During the German offensive of March 1918 the workload greatly increased and involved evacuating patients to No.2 Stationary Hospital at Abbeville. In three days, 1,157 patients were evacuated from Amiens to Abbeville. From 22 to 30 March, 9,243 patients, excluding those from Amiens, were carried. Between November 1916 and March 1918, 113,121 miles had been covered and 36,511 patients carried.

These were used for evacuating sitting patients from hospital trains to hospitals and from there to hospital ships. Between 23 March and 1 April 1918, during the German advance, the buses carried 21,400 patients. Routine servicing and maintenance was carried out at the Audax Motor Works and major repairs and overhauls at the 2nd Repair Shop at Rouen.

813 (MT) Coy ASC (47th Auxiliary Ambulance Car Company) received two Daimler buses on 4 December 1916 and

The omnibus was also used as a mobile pigeon loft. These were operated by the Royal Engineers under the Director of Signals at GHQ. Mobile and static pigeon lofts were established from July 1915 and each army had ten pigeon stations, operated by a sergeant and two corporal despatch riders. The original pigeon lofts had been converted from general service wagon bodies and in late 1916, six buses were converted to complement those already in service. A further six were converted in 1917.

In preparation for the expected German offensive of 1918, 341 Coy ASC, under Major A.H. Lees, was attached to the Auxiliary Omnibus Park, located at Caulieres. The company attached three lorries to each of the seven omnibus companies to carry reserve supplies of petrol for the buses. Forty-four additional lorries carried blankets and baggage for the Divisions to be moved.

During the last few days of March 1918, 211,213 men were transported and 855,638 aggregate miles were covered in an effort that did much to contain the German offensive. The resolve of the men, who drove for sixty

hours at a stretch and the flexibility of the omnibus in moving troops quickly was a major factor in turning the tide and eventually winning the war.

The buses that had been converted to general service lorry bodies were often still referred to as buses by the companies that operated them. They carried everything that the army needed to sustain itself. Companies allotted to Ammunition Parks carried munitions to the frontline trenches, others carried all the food to the men and the letters from home that were so important to morale. These 'frontline' companies were rotated out of the danger areas to allow respite for both men and machines from the shelling of the frontline.

Daily routine was to drive from the lorry park, which may have just been

LGOC B-type, B 2132/LF 8780 after conversion to a pigeon loft. The cages folded flat for travelling and accommodation for two crewmen was built into the rear of the body ~ LTM

ASC bus crews pose in front of their charges at an unknown location ~ LTM

the edge of a road if it was wide enough, or hard standing made up from railway sleepers at the side of the road to a railhead. When loaded, the convoy would set off for their appointed section of frontline for unloading and return to the lorry park empty, or with men returning from the front.

The journey from railhead to trenches could only normally be attempted safely under the cover of darkness. Lights were not permitted as they would be seen by the enemy and would surely result in a bombardment of shells. One night might be clear skies, moonlight and a dry road. The next night might be blackened skies, torrential rain and roads deep in mud.

Often the speed was no more than walking pace as drivers tried to spot pot holes and shell craters in the pitch dark while also trying not to slide off the road in the mud. Columns were halted when the roads became too

dangerous due to enemy shelling, so a day's work might be anything between twelve and twenty-four hours. Often, in times of battle, the drivers had no more time than for a hearty breakfast before starting the next day's work.

It has to be remembered that trenches had no storage facility. Men in the trenches depended on daily deliveries for food and ammunition. It is the first time 'just-in-time' deliveries had been used, certainly on such a huge scale with so much depending on the reliability of supply.

Away from the front, the bulk of the loads carried were road mending materials in support of the Royal Engineers, who were responsible for road making and upkeep. Forestry work kept the lorries busy as forests were felled to become railway sleepers, trench boards, posts for barbed wire, telephone poles and even roadways and hard standing for lorry parks.

Following the Armistice on 11 November 1918, the Auxiliary Omnibus Park was engaged in moving American units and repatriating British prisoners-of-war. In January 1919, thousands of German prisoners-of-war were moved by omnibus from Abbeville to Hesdin.

Nos. 1 and 51 Companies moved to Cologne in January 1919 for the occupation of the Rhineland, although the orders to disband were received in February and they returned to Wissant, near Calais, where 150 buses were selected for repatriation and returned to the streets of London.

It is recorded that one of the buses was independently examined on repatriation and showed very little signs of wear. That is possible as the buses were being overhauled right up to the Armistice and it is quite possible that the examined bus had been overhauled just a few weeks previously.

On 26 April 1918, twenty-one Military Medals were awarded to men of the Auxiliary Omnibus Park, with the Commanding Officer receiving the CMG and the Adjutant the DSO. It seems likely that the medals awarded to the Auxiliary Bus Park were divided equally between the companies and the Commanding Officer in each company nominated individual awards on merit.

For its services during the 1918 offensive that resulted in the Armistice, the Auxiliary Omnibus Park was mentioned, by name, in the despatches of the Commander-in-Chief, Sir Douglas Haig. It was the only Army Service Corps company to be so acknowledged.

In addition to the medals awarded to the Auxiliary Omnibus Park, T.O.T (Train-Omnibus-Tram), the

A B-type is being inspected at an unknown garage following repatriation in early 1919 ~ LTM

A Daimler bus rebodied with a general service body. A toy jester has been mounted on the radiator as a mascot ~ LTM

LGOC staff magazine, provides some information on staff individually recognised for their bravery.

Sergeant Major Matthews MT, ASC, from Mortlake Garage was awarded the French Medaille Militaire and subsequently the British Distinguished Conduct Medal for his actions on 22 January 1916.

He was conveying wounded Tommies during an air raid to Hospital 25 General when a bomb landed on the top deck of his bus. He quickly threw the bomb overboard and as it landed in a ditch it exploded, injuring his knee, hip and breaking his ribs.

Despite his injuries he managed to drive his seventeen passengers to the hospital, where he collapsed in the doorway and was admitted as one of the wounded. He received his decorations in Birmingham from Neville Chamberlain in the presence of the Australian Prime Minister, William Morris Hughes.

In May 1918, the following men were listed as receiving the Military Medal but no details were given:

S. Viner, C.H. Fossy, F.G. Phillips, C.S. Potter, H.J Bender, J. Cummings, T. Blackford, L. Powell, G.R. Membery, W. Strudwick and A.H. Herbert.

M. Johns was awarded the Russian Cross of St George and Conductor J.W. Thames received the Distinguished Conduct Medal.

Troops Carried from the Auxiliary Omnibus Park Records

	Troops Carried	Mileage
July 1917	152,778	418,400
August 1917	212,467	369,040
September 1917	235,593	489,955
October 1917	304,173	582,036
November 1917	229,800	531,101

A MET Daimler and a lorry with a general service body outside Ostend railway station. The lorry appears to be for the servicemen and the bus for civilian refugees ~ LTM

MET Daimler, D155, seen in 1913 at an unknown location in London ~ LTM

Gearless Daimler, D265/LF 9867, in the main square of an unknown Belgian town. The lack of damage and air of normality indicate it is en-route to Antwerp, having only just arrived in Belgium during the early days of the war. The destination boards have been removed and the Dewar's White Label advert remains intact on the upper side ~ LTM

MET Daimler, D219, seen in Antwerp. A badly damaged Daimler stands behind it and the German soldiers and driver indicate that it is one of the many captured by the Germans at Antwerp ~ LTM

A captured Daimler posed with German soldiers in Antwerp shows little damage except for the loss of the destination boards and part of the advertising ~ LTM

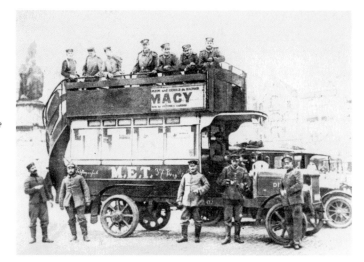

Daimlers from the Royal Naval Division seen at Boulogne alongside a troop train. The registration numbers have been replaced with plates stating 'RND'. The funnels of a passenger ship can be seen in the background ~ LTM

A column of LGOC B-types at an unknown bus park. Note the improvised use of straw to make bonnet covers and canvas protection for the drivers to counter the freezing winter conditions ~ LTM

A column of mixed makes at an unknown base. Three Daimlers stand at the rear behind a 30-cwt Albion, clearly marked WD. The long coats suggest it is wintertime ~ LTM

A column of B-types wait at Grove Park prior to being driven along the A4 trunk road to Avonmouth docks and shipment to France ~ RLCM

A column of buses appear to be posed for the camera with the soldiers on the upper deck all looking towards the camera. The unidentified location is probably Northern France ~ LTM

A busy railhead somewhere in France. The vehicles to the right are loading directly from railway wagons. The B-type in the foreground appears to have a smoky engine and is possibly headed for the assorted supplies being guarded by a rather disinterested looking soldier ~ RL

LGOC B-type seen loading at an unknown railhead with a bus in the background in this rather posed looking photograph somewhere on the Western Front, probably in France ~ RL

Two B-types being loaded with what appears to be sandbags or sacks of grain by Labour Corps personnel from the Empire. The identity numbers on the bonnet sides are War Office numbers, not LGOC fleet numbers ~ RLCM

B-type belonging to 52 MT Coy ASC carrying members of the 1st Indian Cavalry. The driver is posing with the crew wearing a long coat with goggles on his cap. The glass windows are still intact, suggesting this vehicle is far behind the frontlines and has only recently arrived in France ~ LTM

Daimler mobile workshops were allocated to companies for running repairs and servicing. They were fully equipped with machine tools and also capable of undertaking major overhauls ~ LTM

Daimlers were popular with the ASC companies providing transport for the postal service which was run by the Royal Engineers. The banner on the radiator header tank states 'Royal Mail' ~ RLCM

A bus on ambulance duty from 93 Coy ASC collects walking wounded from a casualty clearing station behind the frontlines somewhere on the Somme. The casualties were transferred to a stationary hospital for recuperation before returning to the trenches or repatriation to England for long term convalescence. Note the deep wheel tracks on the frozen ground ~ LTM

A column of buses preparing to embus troops in an unknown Belgian town. Note the damage to the upper deck, although the windows are not boarded up, suggesting they are working away from the Front ~ LTM

Buses returned from war service are being inspected by LGOC managers early in 1919, probably at the LGOC's North Road Coachworks. The LGOC bought back from the War Office buses that were in the best condition for reconditioning and return to service on London's streets ~ LTM

An anti-aircraft gun in the snow. This one is mounted on a Thornycroft chassis and is identical to those mounted on LGOC B-types. The stabiliser legs and drop-sided body were fitted to strengthened chassis by 274 Coy ASC at Plumstead bus garage and the gun was fitted at the Woolwich Arsenal ~ RL

Troops waiting to embus a column of omnibuses somewhere on the Western Front. The forage which can be seen on the driver's canopy was probably for covering the bonnets to protect the engine against the bitter cold when at rest ~ LTM

Daimler, LF 9524, seen in Ghent in September 1914 conveying troops wounded at Antwerp and Belgian refugees. The registration number plate can be seen above the rear window and although the advertising has been removed, the fleet name remains clearly visible ~ LTM

The Home Front

The buses in France are remembered best, but the contribution of the LGOC on what became known as the Home Front cannot be ignored. The population of London more than ever needed a reliable transport service and the increasing needs of the military added to the pressure on services for the Home Front.

In addition to the 1,185 buses sent overseas, 300 were commandeered by the War Office for home use. Lorry bodies were fitted with seating for War Office contracts and to supplement the remaining buses. These were employed mainly to convey workers to factories engaged in war work.

Mounting casualties as the war progressed, meant increasing numbers of wounded were repatriated for treatment and convalescence. LGOC buses were increasingly engaged on the transfer of men from hospital trains to the London hospitals.

Ports were also served by LGOC buses, used as ambulances, for the evacuation of hospital ships to local hospitals. The Chief Constable of Plymouth wrote in November 1915 that the LGOC bus drivers had worked for fourteen months without cause for complaint regarding either their conduct or driving and that there had not been a single accident during that time.

London street scene outside the Bank of England in 1917. The number of omnibuses illustrates how important the role of the LGOC and associated companies was on the Home Front during the war years ~ LTM

AEC Y-type, LU 8035, photographed in June 1919 with a general service lorry body converted for passenger carrying. The notice towards the rear of the body identifies the reduced service route as being to Charing Cross ~ LTM

Servicemen on leave or convalescing were afforded free passage on LGOC buses provided that they were in uniform. Parties of servicemen were conveyed to and from hospitals on an ad hoc basis free of charge. Despite these fares being free gratis, the LGOC meticulously recorded them all and their value was shown in the accounts as donations to charity.

In the half-year to 30 June 1916, the mileage covered conveying non-paying passengers was 2,501 with an estimated cost of £86.12.1. For the half-year to 31 December 1916, the figures were 5,418 miles at £199.19.10. No details are available for the first half of 1917, or 1918. The figures for the half-year to 31 December were 554

miles at £25.13.10., and for 1918, 46 miles at £2.13.5. Belgian refugees were also afforded free travel and for this service the donation to charity amounted to fifty guineas, which was paid to the War Refugees Committee.

Five of the LGOC's London garages were commandeered for War Office use as was the small outpost in Bedford. The loss of Plumstead, Camberwell, Catford, Tottenham and Shepherds Bush garages would have been more keenly felt had a third of the fleet not been commandeered.

Losing a third of the fleet must have resulted in the LGOC having vacant space at garages with the probable closure of some. Although not necessarily the garages of the LGOC's choosing, the rental revenue from the War Office for commandeered garages would have been welcomed. Their loss obviously resulted in some disruption, causing the re-routing of some services and the cancellation of others. Often the re-routing of services was dependent on the locations of factories engaged on war work.

Catford garage was taken over as a repair depot and there was an ASC Driver Training Centre established at Catford and, though not confirmed, the LGOC garage would seem the obvious and ideal place to form the driving school. The LGOC received £1500pa rent for Catford garage with the War Office responsible for all running costs.

The garage at Warner Road, Camberwell, which had capacity for

150 buses was taken over as a reception centre for new vehicles. New vehicles were delivered to Camberwell for inspection and any minor repairs before being allocated to ASC companies. By December 1914 the volume of new vehicles had become too great for the available space at the garage and the reception centre was transferred to Kempton Park Racecourse. On 14 December, Camberwell garage became an ASC repair depot.

In September 1915, the ASC Prisoners-of-War Fund, Mrs Landon's Fund for Horse Transport and Supply Details and the Commercial Motor Fund for Comforts of Men of the Mechanical Transport amalgamated into the ASC Central Comforts Fund. In 1917 the fund became an Authorised Association and Warner Road became the store and

LGOC B-type, B 592/LE 9119, with windows blown out during an air-raid ~ LTM

A lorry-bus showing the steps arrangement. The 'General' name stands out clearly on the sides along with the temporary destination boards showing the reduced service against the otherwise drab wartime livery ~ LTM

packing depot. The Borough of Camberwell suspended the payment of rates at the War Office's request. The War Office paid £1350pa rent for Warner Road garage plus £118pa for the use of furniture and also paid all day-to-day running costs.

The garage at King's Highway, Plumstead, which had only been opened on 15 October 1913, was commandeered on 8 March 1915. It was for the use of 274 Coy ASC, which was the company responsible for the transport needs of the Woolwich Arsenal and Dockyard. The rent for Plumstead garage was £1259pa plus £131pa for the use of furniture and

equipment with all running costs the responsibility of the War Office.

The Woolwich Arsenal employed a workforce of 80,000 people during the war years. All required bussing in from around the capital and outlying areas and the loss of Plumstead garage must have been the most keenly felt.

Previously 274 Coy ASC had been based at Grove Park until the workload became too great to be serviced from there. Plumstead garage was only one mile from the Arsenal, which greatly reduced dead mileage and the garage provided garaging and workshop facilities for the 122 heavy lorries, 101 light lorries and vans, nine steam lorries and fourteen light cars employed by 274 Coy ASC.

The company was also used as a finishing school for newly trained drivers from Osterley Park and other London training schools before they were sent overseas. The workshop facilities at the garage were used to train mechanics before they were transferred to work in the increasingly busy ASC repair shops in France.

The former New Central Omnibus Company garage at Bedford was commandeered as the headquarters of 373 Coy ASC in October 1915. 373 Coy was responsible for general transport duties for the whole of Eastern Command. The vehicle strength rose from an original 240 to 2,000, with some 400 based at Bedford and the others at sub-stations throughout the Home Counties and East Anglia.

The workshops were used for the maintenance of forty ambulances. These were owned by the British Red Cross Society and loaned to the government which was responsible for their running costs.

352 Coy ASC was formed at Bedford on 25 April 1915 and the garage was used for repair of vehicles, basic training of new recruits and for training mechanics and drivers. The company moved to Bristol in June 1915 before embarking at Avonmouth for France.

The Ministry of Munitions decided in 1918 that 606 Coy ASC would take over the transport needs of the Aircraft Department. This entailed an increase of 170 vehicles and workshops and

Munitions production at Chiswick garage after being taken over by the Ministry of Munitions ~ LTM

Bodies in store, probably at LGOC's North Road Coachworks. The left one, marked EST & Co., is from East Surrey Traction Co Ltd., who had close links with LGOC from 1914 ~ LTM

stores were established at the LGOC's garage in Goldhawk Road, Shepherds Bush, West London.

None of the garages commandeered were large enough to garage all the vehicles of the respective ASC companies. They would therefore have been the headquarters and workshops of the companies with the majority of the vehicles parked at the factory premises that they were serving, or in the surrounding streets. The military were certainly not shy of using public roads for parking at the time.

In addition to the five garages commandeered by the ASC, Chiswick garage was taken over for munitions manufacture. It is not known why Tottenham garage was commandeered.

The LGOC was faced with providing a reliable and growing service to the increasing number of factories engaged in work for the Ministry of War with a reduced fleet of vehicles and staff numbers. This unenviable task became more difficult in August 1916 with the introduction of rationing as German submarines in the English Channel increasingly disrupted petrol supplies.

Rationing led to many of the older buses being withdrawn from service and various experiments were conducted with substitute fuels, particularly gas, though without much success. To help lessen the impact of reduced capacity and heavier workload, the Metropolitan Police granted permission for standing passengers on the lower deck.

In July 1918, existing contracts with the Shell petroleum company were cancelled. Subsequent petrol was drawn from government controlled 'POOL' petrol at a price determined by the government.

Behind the Scenes

Buses and the requisitioning of garages are the visible evidence of the LGOC's war effort. However, no less valuable contributions were made away from the public gaze.

All LGOC garages and coachworks were declared to be War Office Controlled Establishments on 3 December 1915. This appears to have made no practical difference as LGOC managers and staff were retained. It did give the War Office control over routes which could be changed to serve factories engaged on war work, particularly the munitions production at the Woolwich Arsenal.

The LGOC involvement in the war effort was by no means entirely based on patriotism. The company received substantial financial reward for their cooperation with the War Office. The LGOC received £450,000 from the War Office in 1915.

In April 1916, a further £585,000 was received. This had been reduced from the LGOC invoice for £626,000 by the War Office in respect to the LGOC keeping the bodies of buses. This must have been for the buses converted to general service bodies before being taken over by the War Office and probably the 200 buses returned by the War Office in October 1915.

The apparent lengthy delay in receiving payment was not unusual. A common complaint about the subsidy schemes and commandeered vehicles was that the War Office delayed payment for as long as possible. These delays were more likely caused by the

Daimler converted to a general service body and covered in mud somewhere in Europe ~ RL

Army Service Corps trainees, probably at Hounslow garage. The LGOC instructors can be seen wearing white coats and a Belsize lorry stands in Bay 3 facing the camera behind men inspecting a dismantled rear axle ~ LTM

Treasury than the War Office, who themselves complained of the difficulty in obtaining money from the Treasury to fund the subsidy schemes.

The amounts paid would appear too high for the number of vehicles, so presumably included rent for garages, payment for munitions and bus services. Other services included the instruction of drivers and mechanics and garage management training.

The expansion of the Walthamstow factory to allow the installation of the moving track production line in 1916 was partly funded by War Office grants. This track increased the number of vehicles produced for the War Office, from thirty to forty-five per week. Initially these were Daimlers and, from December 1917, AEC Y-types following the ending of the agreement between AEC and Daimler.

By 1911, the military were responsible for a growing fleet of motor vehicles and had recognised the future need for repair facilities on a large scale. The LGOC, with its large fleet and well established garage and repair facilities, were the obvious place to seek guidance for establishing workshops.

In 1911, two officers from the ASC Training Establishment were attached to the LGOC to learn garage management. The number of ASC officers attached to LGOC garages for training continued to grow through subsequent years.

Subsequently, the ASC Repair Depots established in France for the maintenance of motor vehicles were set up using the LGOC working practices as a model. These Repair Depots were essential in keeping the constantly increasing numbers of lorries, buses, ambulances and the thousands of horse-drawn wagons operational.

Staff losses had initially been balanced with the loss of vehicles, however, as the war escalated, so did the need for volunteers and, from January 1916, conscripted men for service overseas. In addition to losing drivers, skilled mechanics were urgently needed for the repair shops and mobile workshop units of the ASC companies in France and Flanders to service the ASC's rapidly growing fleet of motor lorries.

Published numbers vary regarding the staff that served in the military during the war. The LGOC Board Minutes record that the men enlisted from all the companies of the Underground Electric Railways Company of London (UERL) was 15,750 men.

Of these, 469 were killed in action, 475 were wounded, thirty-one were listed as missing and seventy became prisoners-of-war. Eighty-two per cent of the enlisted men returned to work for the UERL after discharge. In October 1918, there were 5,000 LGOC men recorded in the minutes as serving with the military.

These shortages led to the use of women conductors and cleaners for the first time in 1916 when 200 women were taken on for training in February. The LGOC employed a total of 4,600 women during the war years. All the women were dismissed when the war ended as the jobs of the enlisted men had been kept open for their return.

Following agreement with the London and Provincial Union of Licensed

Women cleaners were recruited to replace the men who enlisted. These four are seen posing by their sparkling bus at Willesden garage ~ LTM

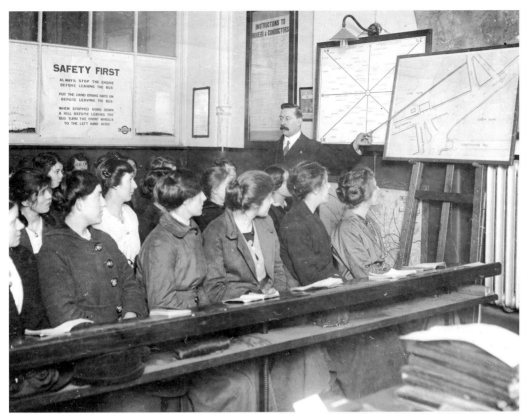

New recruits receiving route training at the LGOC Training Centre in Milman's Street, Chelsea, London, SW10 ~ LTM

Vehicle Workers, staff employed in the LGOC coachworks received a 'War Bonus'. This was extended to all staff and increased at regular intervals for the duration of the war.

The bonus increased wages to counteract the rising cost of living caused by the war. Income tax increased from 9d (3.75p) in the pound in 1914 to 6s (30p) in the pound by 1918. A 4d (1.6p) loaf of bread in 1914 had increased in price to 1s (5p) by 1917 when the government introduced a subsidy which reduced it to 9d.

The LGOC invested regularly in Government War Loans and set up a Staff War Loans agreement whereby staff had two shillings deducted weekly from their wages which was put into the War Loans Fund. Most of what had been given as War Bonus was effectively redirected to the Treasury.

Many of the men enlisting for the ASC at Grove Park had never driven before and, initially, LGOC driving instructors were employed at Grove Park. The need for trained drivers quickly outgrew the facilities at Grove Park and a training centre was established at the London United Tramways depot at Hounslow. This facility was extended to Osterley Park, a few miles to the west, in May 1915. It was initially administered by the LGOC who employed 100 of their own instructors and drivers as trainers. They had at their disposal a training fleet, owned by the War Office, of 320 vehicles from eighteen different manufacturers. These included Leyland, Karrier, Commer, Daimler, Wolseley, Peerless, Dennis, Belsize, Halley, Albion, Straker-Squire, Pagefield, Hallford, Berna, and LGOC.

The work of the training school must have felt very different to the instructors. The LGOC training school was at Chelsea, where the emphasis was on safety and providing a courteous service to the public. Even in these early days of public transport, the LGOC recognised the benefits of a good public image. Driving courses lasted for a minimum of five weeks.

The military required quantity, not quality, and the emphasis was on drivers who were competent as quickly as possible. Newly qualified drivers

were expected to be produced within days rather than weeks. The LGOC appears to have had difficulty in managing this reduction in standards and time available for training. Too often, instructors found it impossible to lower the standards they had so rigidly enforced at the Chelsea training school.

On 7 May, 1917 the running of the Training School was taken over and administered by the military, resulting in a fifty per cent increase in trainees passing through the school. Each new recruit had to learn to drive four different makes of vehicle, by day and by night, around training circuits that included Marble Arch, Pall Mall and Hyde Park.

Training was conducted using fully laden vehicles after it was found that drivers trained on empty vehicles were

Women recruits at Milman's Street being fitted out with their new uniforms ~ LTM

Eighty-nine new conductors are proudly photographed after their one week's training at Milman's Street Training Centre. A recruitment poster on the side of the omnibus offers ten hour shifts for six days each week ~ LTM

unable to cope with laden vehicles. Newly qualified drivers were attached to Home Front ASC companies for practical experience before being deployed overseas.

Between May 1915 and June 1917, 23,580 men passed the driver training course and 1,036 were deemed unsuitable and returned to Grove Park for light car training. A further 2,435 men were deemed unsuitable for any driving and posted to the infantry, or as packers and loaders in the ASC.

On a single day in May 1916, 879 drivers were tested after their course. In the same month, 24,212 men were engaged in driver training at Osterley Park and other London training centres, particularly Catford.

The LGOC never forgot its staff serving overseas and regular copies of T.O.T. (Train – Omnibus – Tram), the staff magazine, were sent to the Western Front. It is clear from correspondence in the magazines that these were eagerly looked forward to and a great boost to morale.

Neither were the men's families forgotten. No details exist in the Board Minutes, but letters of appreciation appear in T.O.T. for the subsidy paid to the men's families while they were away and for the regular day trips organised by the LGOC for the families separated from their serving menfolk.

The London General Omnibus Company and its staff had every reason to feel proud at the end of the war.

Three reconditioned Daimlers with general service bodies seen displayed for sale after the war. The London and Kent civilian registration numbers are from 1913, 1914 and 1915 and indicate that all three lorries were in service on the Home Front ~ LTM

LGOC B-type, LF 9287, from Palmers Green garage conveys City of London policemen to the recruiting office ~ LTM

B-type, B1767/LF 8540, conveying wounded servicemen. The men on the upper deck are carrying crutches and the presence of nurses suggest the photograph was taken at a London hospital. LGOC operated a free service for servicemen to and from hospital during the war years ~ LTM

The last of the women conductors employed during the war years, Ellen Bulfield, hands over her bus for the last time. All the women employed by the LGOC to replace the men on military service were dismissed when the men returned from the war ~ LTM

Women mechanics work on a bus chassis at an unknown LGOC garage ~ LTM

A busy LGOC workshop with women mechanics refurbishing rear axles ~ LTM

Daimlers with War Office specification general service goods bodies outside the LGOC's North Road Coachworks in Highbury, North London ~ LTM

The seating arrangement for the Daimler lorry/buses seen outside the North Road Coachworks ~ LTM

LGOC bodybuilders work on a general service body at the North Road Coachworks. Many bus bodies were replaced with general service bodies and LGOC built the bodies for the new chassis built by AEC at the Walthamstow works ~ LTM

His Majesty King George V inspects a B-type chassis on a visit to an unidentified LGOC garage ~ LTM

The King watches a woman machinist who appears to be employed on armaments manufacture, possibly at Chiswick garage. The darkness of the photograph is an indication of the poor lighting conditions at factories and workshops at the time ~ LTM

B-type chassis awaiting reconditioning after re-purchase from the War Office following their return from France. Those in the background still retain their bodies, though in a very dilapidated state ~ LTM

AEC Y-type lorry-bus, CS/31, on the Hampstead Heath to Pimlico route. The body has seating for 27 passengers and the signs on the body advertise the reduced service on the route. It remained in service until January 1920 ~ LTM

Army Service Corps personnel receiving training using an LGOC B-type. The position of the gear lever and handbrake made entry to the cab easier from the passenger side, which possibly explains the unusual fixed wooden boards on this very unusual style cab ~ LTM

B-types on Private Hire work outside the British Club for Belgian Soldiers in Connaught Street, Bayswater. The bandsmen are from the 1st Regiment of the Belgian Caribineers ~ LTM

The LGOC bus garage in Warner Road, Camberwell, which had capacity for 150 omnibuses. It was commandeered for use as a reception centre for new vehicles in 1914 before becoming a repair depot in December 1914 when the workload became too great and the reception centre was relocated to Kempton Park Racecourse ~ LTM

Women conductors take a break in the canteen at Kensal Rise bus garage. The menu board offers a choice of five cooked meals and four hot desserts ~ LTM

WOMEN WANTED AS OMNIBUS CONDUCTORS

HEIGHT OVER 5FT. AGE 20 TO 35 APPLY L.G.O.CO. MILMAN'S ST. CHELSEA S.W.

Recruitment poster for women conductors ~ LTM

Walthamstow and AEC

The factory stood at the corner of Blackhorse Lane and Hookers Lane, now the site of Forest Works Industrial Estate, Walthamstow, London E17. It had been commissioned by Arthur Salisbury-Jones, head of the Vanguard Company to build buses for the Motor Omnibus Construction Co. (MOC)

MOC was wound up and the LGOC acquired the works when it took over Vanguard in 1908. When the LGOC was taken over by the Underground Electric Railways Company in 1912, a wholly owned subsidiary company, The Associated Equipment Company Ltd., was formed to undertake the manufacturing work of the LGOC. Walter James Iden replaced Frank

Searle as chief engineer in 1911 and continued in this role until 1917.

The new company, AEC, continued building the B-type for the LGOC and reached an agreement with Daimler for them to be the sole selling agent for vehicles outside of the needs of the LGOC. By 1913, this included the fitting of Daimler engines into a modified LGOC chassis - the Daimler B-type. The B-Type was also built with 'Associated Equipment Co' script, instead of LGOC script on the radiator header tank, though it is not known how many carried AEC radiators. War Office records also suggest that some of the Walthamstow built Daimlers carried AEC radiators.

AEC B-type, B 2576, heads a batch of chassis outside the works in Blackhorse Lane en-route to the coachworks in 1912. Registered LF 9711, it served with the MET company and is believed to have remained in London throughout the war ~ LTM

Driver, Walter John Cornell, stands by the front wheel of B-type, B186/LC 3824. Allocated to Cricklewood garage, it was ordered in 1910 and one of a batch delivered between January and March 1911 ~ LTM

Most of the B-types impressed by the War Office were buses, although some were either built, or rebodied with general service bodies as lorries. While there is little doubt about the ability of the buses when used as buses, there is a question mark about the suitability of the B-type when used as a lorry for active service in France.

That may be because of the extra cargo space and weight the lorry body permitted, or the transmission being designed for the stop/start journeys of urban street work and not the constant running of longer distance rural work. That would have resulted in the B-type having to work harder to keep up with columns of mixed makes of lorry and was one of the deficiencies highlighted

during the War Office trial in 1912. It should also be remembered that the bus drivers were experienced men and the lorry drivers could often be newly trained. An experienced driver with a cargo of live men will naturally be more sympathetic to his vehicle than an inexperienced driver with a load that can't repay a particularly rough ride.

It is recorded that vibration caused the front engine mounting bolts to regularly fail, resulting in engine main bearings failing. Whatever the reason, the war diary of 67 Coy ASC records, 'the LGOC required more time and attention than it was worth'.

It would seem that the LGOCs supplied to the war effort were ones already in civilian service. AEC production during the war years was predominantly Daimlers for the War Office in 3, 4 and 5-ton variants. AEC built the chassis using engines bought from Daimler, who then bought the completed vehicle back from AEC and sold them to the War Office.

This arrangement continued until 1915, when the passing of the Munitions of War Act 1915 made the Walthamstow factory a Government Controlled Establishment. AEC came under direct Government control on 30 June 1916 and from then received the engines from the War Office and supplied new Daimlers directly to the War Office. The five year agreement with Daimler ended in December 1917 and was not renewed.

During 1916 work was undertaken on the design of a new model specifically to meet the requirements of the War Office. This was the Y-type and although some AEC ideas were incorporated it adhered to the same War Office specification for the 'Subsidy Model' produced by other makers - Thornycroft, Leyland, Dennis, Maudslay, etc.

In January 1917, the Y-type lorry, previously built with Daimler engines, began using a Tylor engine and an AEC radiator replaced the Daimler one. By the Armistice in 1918, 5,200 Y-Types had been built.

LGOC lorries, whilst mainly built with general service bodies were also used as field kitchens, armoured cars, field workshops and anti-aircraft gun carriers. The boiler plate bodywork for the armoured cars was designed by Felix Samson and fitted by the shipbuilding firm of Forges et Chantiers de France at Dunkirk. They proved to be too heavy and slow compared to the armoured Rolls Royces, so were rarely used in action.

AEC Y-type built at Walthamstow with the War Office general service body probably built at the LGOC's North Road Coachworks ~ TG

Daimler mobile workshop with the sides open showing the comprehensive range of Drummond machine tools that provided the ability to carry out major overhauls as well as routine servicing and maintenance ~ RLCM

Anti-aircraft guns were fitted at Woolwich Arsenal, after the lorry chassis had been reinforced and reconditioned by 274 Coy ASC in the workshops at Plumstead garage. The body sides were hinged to fold flat, creating a large platform for the gunners to work on and stabilising legs were fitted. On completion, 274 Coy drivers drove them to Avonmouth docks for shipment to France.

Both LGOCs and Daimlers were converted to mobile workshops. These were allocated to all ASC companies for running repairs and stayed with the company whenever they moved. They also undertook major rebuilds and complete overhauls when required.

The basis for a travelling workshop was a box body fitted to a standard chassis. The sides and rear of the body were split horizontally half way between roof and floor. All three bottom halves could be folded down to double the size of the platform onto sturdy, adjustable legs.

The upper sides were hinged at the roof and could be opened to provide a canopy for the work area and sometimes contained windows, which provided additional light when the body was open. There was virtually no room to work when the body was closed for travelling.

A lathe, milling and drilling machines, vice bench, grindstone, small forge and anvil were fitted to the floor of the workshop. A carpenter's bench, bandsaw and a comprehensive range of hand tools completed the equipment.

These machine tools were powered by electric motors, served by a dynamo which was powered by a separate petrol engine, usually of Austin manufacture, or sometimes by a belt arrangement from the lorry's engine. This independent power supply allowed the workshops to be used as totally stand-alone units wherever they were needed. Spare parts were carried amongst the machine tools, on the roof or in a separate vehicle.

The machine tools were built by Drummond of Guildford and the workshops were equipped to War Office design and specification.

In May 1917, a new assembly hall was completed at Walthamstow, housing a 265ft long assembly track. Based on the pioneering design by Henry Ford in Detroit, U.S.A., this assembly line increased production from thirty to forty-five complete vehicles per week.

It was the first time a continuous production line had been used in Britain. The cost of building the track and the extensions needed to house it was £63,970 and it attracted a Government grant of £26,400.

AEC built more than vehicles. From July 1916, 4.5" Mk VII shells were manufactured at Walthamstow for the Ministry of Munitions. By the end of 1917, 53,312 shells had been produced, earning AEC £90,841, the equivalent of ninety Y-types at the 1918 retail price.

A column of B-types at an unknown base in 1915. War Office number 3097 has an AEC badge and stands alongside one with an LGOC badge on the radiator. The upward facing arrow signifies that it is government property ~ RLCM

A column of AEC Y-types in service with the American Army. The vehicles carry American identity numbers and are seen on an American base somewhere on the Western Front ~ RL

Daimlers built at Walthamstow are seen here in ranks at Kempton Park Racecourse to the west of London, prior to allocation the whichever ASC company was to operate them. Kempton Park became the new vehicle receiving depot when Camberwell LGOC garage became too small in December 1914 ~ RLCM

An AEC Y-type is flanked by a Belsize on the left and a Pierce Arrow while loading cases of spare parts destined for France at the Short's Gardens spare parts receiving and distribution depot near Covent Garden, London. ~ RLCM

The Memorial Window at the Garrison Church of Saint Martin Longmoor

The London Passenger Transport Board offered to provide this stained glass window to complement four windows commemorating the railway companies.

St Paul holds St Paul's Cathedral and St Edward the Confessor of Westminster holds Westminster Abbey. The coats of arms of London, London County Council and the counties served by the Board surround the figures.

The inscription at the bottom reads

TO THE GLORY OF GOD & in grateful memory of the Constituent Companies of the London Transport Passenger Board who fell in the Great War 1914-1919

Martin Travers was commissioned to design and build the five windows, which were dedicated on 7 May 1939.

Auxiliary Omnibus Company
Military Medal Awards

Pte. Benjamin Leverton	M1/6387	1st Auxiliary Bus Coy
Pte. Frank Montgomery	M1/6250	1st Auxiliary Bus Coy
C.S.M. Albert Wellbelove	M/32252	1st Auxiliary Bus Coy
Pte. Arthur Morris	M1/6826	2nd Auxiliary Bus Coy
Pte. John Blackie	M1/09171	2nd Auxiliary Bus Coy
Sgt. Frederick Keene	C/3003	2nd Auxiliary Bus Coy
Pte. Frederick Palmer	M2/115456	15th Auxiliary Bus Coy
Pte. John Camp	M2/115811	15th Auxiliary Bus Coy
Cpl. Frederick Jackson	M2/104393	15th Auxiliary Bus Coy
Pte. Leonard Richardson	M2/046487	16th Auxiliary Bus Coy
Sgt. Charles Fox	M2/119422	16th Auxiliary Bus Coy
Cpl. Samuel Plevey	M2/050671	16th Auxiliary Bus Coy
Pte. David Jones	M2/121922	18th Auxiliary Bus Coy
Sgt. Percival Bridge	M2/115464	18th Auxiliary Bus Coy
Cpl. Reginald Carpenter	M/32539	18th Auxiliary Bus Coy
Pte. Donald Hesketh	M/321094	50th Auxiliary Bus Coy
Cpl. Bertie Major	MS/4279	50th Auxiliary Bus Coy
Cpl. Gilbert Calder	M/033755	50th Auxiliary Bus Coy
Pte. Robert Ferguson	M2/136330	51st Auxiliary Bus Coy
Sgt. George Staynes	M2/113196	51st Auxiliary Bus Coy
Sgt. Ernest Campling	M2/106457	51st Auxiliary Bus Coy

Bibliography

Army Service Corps archives ~ Royal Logistic Corps Museum

London Transport archives ~ London Transport Museum

The Royal Army Service Corps ~ Col R.H. Beadon

Army Service Corps ~ Col M. Young

Transportation on the Western Front ~ Col A.M. Henniker

The Motorbus in War ~ A.M. Beatson

The AEC Story part 1 ~ B. Thackray

AEC Vehicles – Origins to 1929 ~ B. Thackray

The London B Type Motor Omnibus ~ G.J. Robbins & J.B. Atkinson

London General ~ London Transport

AEC - Builders of London's Buses ~ A. Thomas & J. Aldridge

The London Motor Bus 1896-1962 ~ R.W. Kidner

Military Transport of WW1 ~ C. Ellis & D. Bishop

Early Armoured Cars ~ E. Bartholomew

The Omnibus ~ J. Hibbs (editor)

The Commercial Motor